Baby Giraffes

Bobbie Kalman

🌲 Crabtree Publishing Company

www.crabtreebooks.com

It's fun to learn about Baby Animals

Created by Bobbie Kalman

Dedicated by Michael Golka
To Amber—stretch your youth to its fullest
Love, Dad

**Author and
Editor-in-Chief**
Bobbie Kalman

Editor
Kathy Middleton

Proofreader
Crystal Sikkens

Photo research
Bobbie Kalman

Production coordinator
Katherine Berti

Design
Bobbie Kalman
Katherine Berti
Samantha Crabtree (cover)

Illustrations
Katherine Berti: page 12

Photographs
Digital Vision: pages 14, 21 (top)
Shutterstock: cover, pages 1, 3, 4, 5, 6, 7,
8, 9, 10, 11, 12, 13, 15, 16, 17, 18,
19, 20, 21 (bottom), 22, 23, 24

Library and Archives Canada Cataloguing in Publication

Kalman, Bobbie, 1947-
    Baby giraffes / Bobbie Kalman.

(It's fun to learn about baby animals)
Includes index.
ISBN 978-0-7787-3961-6 (bound).--ISBN 978-0-7787-3980-7 (pbk.)

    1. Giraffe--Infancy--Juvenile literature. I. Title.
II. Series: It's fun to learn about baby animals

QL737.U56K354 2010   j599.638'139   C2009-905193-1

Library of Congress Cataloging-in-Publication Data

Kalman, Bobbie.
    Baby giraffes / Bobbie Kalman.
        p. cm. -- (It's fun to learn about baby animals)
    Includes index.
    ISBN 978-0-7787-3980-7 (pbk. : alk. paper) -- ISBN 978-0-7787-3961-6
(reinforced library binding : alk. paper)
    1. Giraffe--Juvenile literature. 2. Giraffe--Infancy--Juvenile literature. I. Title.
II. Series.

QL737.U56K33 2010
599.638'139--dc22
                                                  2009034819

Crabtree Publishing Company

www.crabtreebooks.com   1-800-387-7650

Printed in China/122009/CT20090915

Published in Canada
Crabtree Publishing
616 Welland Ave.
St. Catharines, Ontario
L2M 5V6

Published in the United States
Crabtree Publishing
350 Fifth Ave.
59th floor
New York, NY 10118

Published in the United Kingdom
Crabtree Publishing
Maritime House
Basin Road North, Hove
BN41 1WR

Published in Australia
Crabtree Publishing
386 Mt. Alexander Rd.
Ascot Vale (Melbourne)
VIC 3032

What is in this book?

What is a giraffe?

A giraffe is a **mammal**. Mammals are animals with hair or fur. Giraffes have a thick layer of fur covering their bodies. Mammals are **warm-blooded** animals. Their bodies are warmed from the inside and are always about the same temperature.

Born live

Mammal babies are **born**. Baby giraffes are born. They grow inside the bodies of their mothers and come out live.

Mother's milk

Mammal mothers make milk inside their bodies. Mammal babies drink the milk. Drinking mother's milk is called **nursing**. This giraffe **calf**, or baby, is nursing.

Giant giraffes!

Giraffes are the tallest land animals in the world! **Bulls**, or males, are up to 17 feet (5.2 meters) tall. **Cows**, or females, can be 14 feet (4.3 meters) tall. When they are born, calves, or young giraffes, are 6 feet (1.8 meters) tall.

How tall are they?

The chart on the wall next to this giraffe family shows the **heights** of these giraffes. How tall is each giraffe? How tall are you?

17 feet
5.2 M

14.8 feet
4.5 M

14 feet
4.3 M

7 feet
2.1 M

6 feet
1.8 M

This giraffe mother is very tall. Her calf will grow to be as tall as she is.

The giraffe family

There are several kinds of giraffes. Four are shown on the next page. The animal shown in the picture below is called an okapi. Okapis also belong to the giraffe family, but they look more like zebras.

The okapi is related to a giraffe. Its neck is long, but it is not as long as a giraffe's neck.

reticulated giraffe

South African giraffe

Masai giraffe

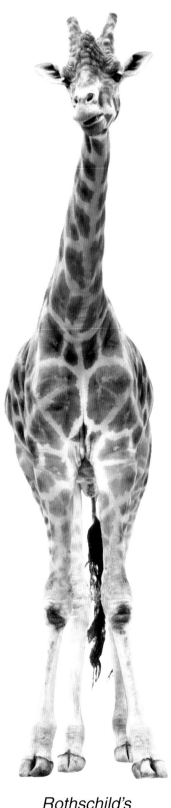

Rothschild's giraffe

9

Coats with spots

A giraffe's coat has brown spots. The spots have cream-colored lines between them. Some giraffe coats have thick lines between the spots. These giraffe calves have thick lines between their spots.

These giraffes are reticulated giraffes.

This calf and cow have spots with smooth

edges. The lines between the spots are thin.

No two giraffes have the same **pattern** of spots.

A pattern is colors and shapes that repeat.

A giraffe's body

Giraffes are **vertebrates**. Vertebrates are animals with **backbones**. Backbones are the bones in the middle of an animal's back. A vertebrate has many other bones inside its body, too. The bones make up a **skeleton**.

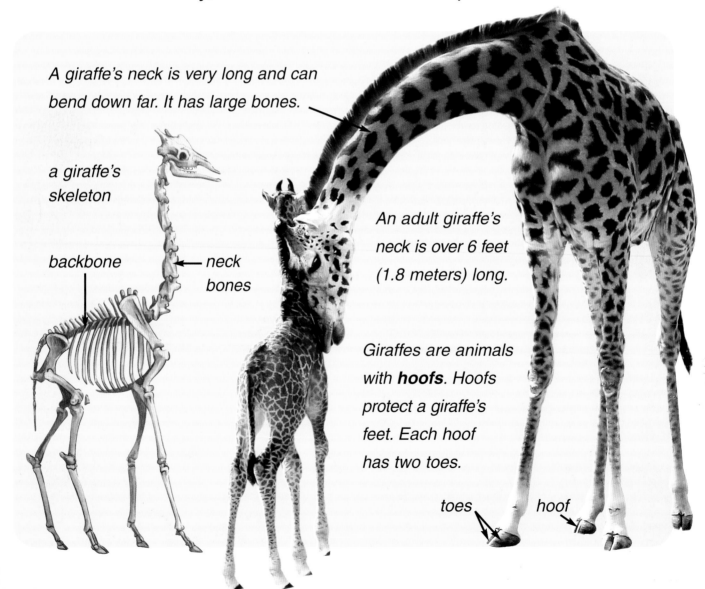

A giraffe's neck is very long and can bend down far. It has large bones.

a giraffe's skeleton

backbone

neck bones

An adult giraffe's neck is over 6 feet (1.8 meters) long.

*Giraffes are animals with **hoofs**. Hoofs protect a giraffe's feet. Each hoof has two toes.*

toes

hoof

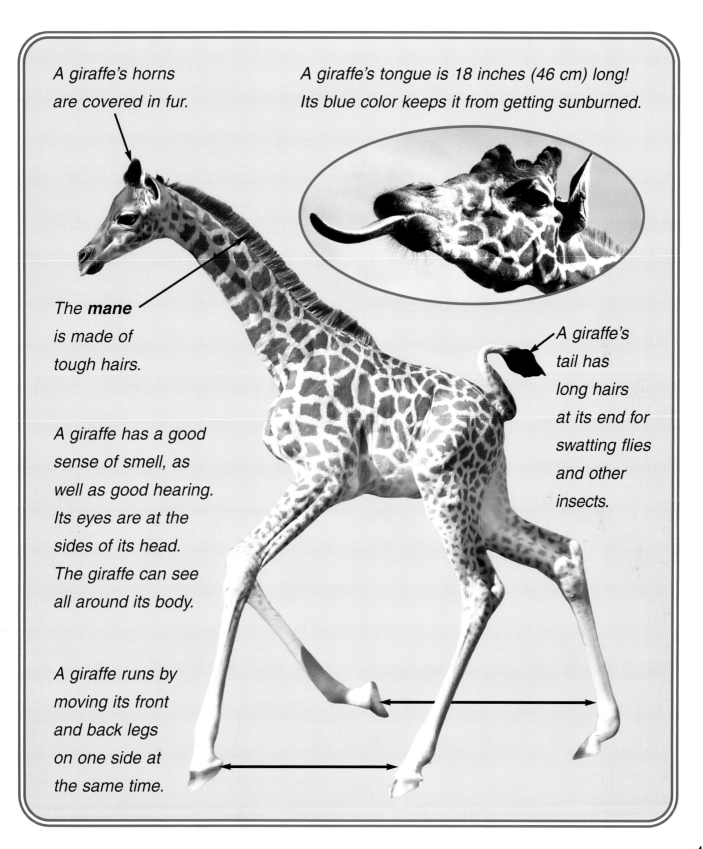

A giraffe's horns are covered in fur.

A giraffe's tongue is 18 inches (46 cm) long! Its blue color keeps it from getting sunburned.

The **mane** is made of tough hairs.

A giraffe's tail has long hairs at its end for swatting flies and other insects.

A giraffe has a good sense of smell, as well as good hearing. Its eyes are at the sides of its head. The giraffe can see all around its body.

A giraffe runs by moving its front and back legs on one side at the same time.

Giraffe habitats

A long time ago, giraffes lived in many places. Today, they live only in some parts of Africa. Their **habitats** are the **woodlands** and **savannas** of Africa. Habitats are natural areas where animals live. Woodlands are areas with many trees. Savannas are hot, grassy habitats with bushes and a few trees.

Giraffes do not need to drink water every day. They get water from the leaves they eat. Water holes are dangerous places for giraffe calves. Lions, hyenas, and leopards hunt baby giraffes there. The less a giraffe needs to drink, the safer it is.

lion

leopard

hyena

Predators hunt and eat other animals. Lions, leopards, and hyenas are predators that hunt giraffes.

A giraffe's life cycle

This mother giraffe is carrying a baby giraffe inside her body.

A mother giraffe carries her baby inside her body for about fifteen months. When the baby is ready to be born, it drops out of its mother's body and falls to the ground. The mother stands while the baby is born. Within one hour, the baby gets up and starts nursing.

A baby giraffe looks just like its mother, but it is much smaller.

This baby giraffe was just born. Its mother is cleaning its fur. The calf will grow quickly. When a female giraffe is between three and four years old, she can have babies. Each time a baby is born, a new **life cycle** begins. A life cycle is the set of changes an animal goes through from the time it is born to the time it becomes an adult and can make babies.

Food for calves

Giraffes are **herbivores**. Herbivores are animals that eat mainly plants. Giraffes eat the buds and leaves of trees. A baby giraffe drinks only milk for the first week of its life. It then starts eating some plants. The calf keeps nursing, as well, until it is over a year old.

Giraffes are so tall that they can reach trees that other animals cannot reach. Even baby giraffes, such as this one, can eat the leaves of tall trees! Their favorite trees are acacia trees. Acacia trees have a lot of **thorns**. Thorns are sharp, like needles.

19

Giraffe herds

Giraffes live in groups called **herds**. A herd can have between four and fifty giraffes. Living in herds is safer for giraffes with calves. The adult giraffes protect the babies from predators.

calf

baby

Some herds are made up of cows and their calves. The second giraffe in this herd has a baby in her body. The calf in the picture belongs to another mother. It was just born.

Baby giraffes are part of **crèche**, or nursery, groups. A mother giraffe watches over all the calves while the other mothers find food. The mothers take turns babysitting.

Neck messages

Giraffes use their long necks to reach food in tall trees. Giraffes also use their necks in other ways.

(A)

Which giraffes are using their necks to:
1. fight
2. play
3. see predators far away
4. show love

Answers:
1—D; 2—A;
3—B; 4—C

Words to Know and Index

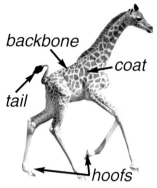

backbone
coat
tail
hoofs

bodies
pages 4, 5,
12–13, 16, 21

food
pages 18–19,
21, 22

height
pages 6–7

herds
pages 20–21

Masai giraffes
page 9

messages
pages 22–23

nursing
pages 5, 16, 18

**reticulated
giraffes**
pages 9, 11

**Rothschild's
giraffes** page 9

**South African
giraffes** page 9